MAKE MONEY BLOGGING ON WORDPRESS

THE ULTIMATE GUIDE TO CREATING A PROFITABLE BLOG.

TOVAL EZEANI

WWW.TOVALEZEANI.COM

COPYRIGHT & DISCLOSURES

COPYRIGHT © 2020

All rights reserved. No part of this publication may be reproduced, distributed, stored in a retrieval system, or transmitted in any form or by any means, including photocopying, recording, or other electronic or mechanical methods, without the prior written permission of the author, except by reviewers who may quote brief passages in a review.

FOR PERMISSION REQUESTS, PLEASE EMAIL: TOVAL@TOVALEZEANI.COM

This book contains some affiliate links, meaning the author receives a referral fee on any purchase at no extra expense to the purchaser.

PRINTED VERSION LINKS

All the links in this book had been numbered and published on www.tovalezeani.com/booklinks[1] for the convenience of paperback readers.

CONTENTS

Introduction   5

SECTION 1 - SETTING UP YOUR BLOG
1. Niche Selection   13
2. Web Hosting   20
3. WordPress and Theme Installations   28
4. Securing and Enhancing Your Blog with Plugins   36
5. Basic SEO: How to Rank Higher on Google   39

SECTION 2 - BUILD YOUR TRIBE
6. Content Strategy That Fuels Sales   51
7. Content SEO Optimization   61
8. Driving Traffic To Your Blog   71
9. Building Your Email List   78

SECTION 3 - MONETIZATION
10. Blog Monetization Methods   91
11. How to Make Selling Natural And Not Annoying To Your Audience   100

Conclusion   107
THANK YOU FOR READING   111
About The Author   113
References   115

INTRODUCTION

Is blogging still a viable business? Can I make money through blogging? Why should people read my blog when there are millions of other blogs on the same topic? Those are normally the thoughts of beginner bloggers.

If those are thoughts going through your mind now, let me confidently tell you, yes blogging is still a viable business today and will continue to be in years to come. The only first action you need to take to get going is to take off your cloak of self-doubt as I did.

Yes I know there are millions of blogs in my niche but mine will succeed! I'm going to be that distinctive refreshing voice in my chosen niche that my readers can't get enough of.

These affirmative words backed with proven action methods are what this book is all about. Have you ever wondered why there are so many musicians and many more coming out daily singing mostly love/relationship songs and we still listen, enjoy and buy them? It is because each musician has his or her distinctive voice and style and that is what keeps the fans raving. So are you, no matter how many blogs exist out there, your fans are waiting out there to read your blog. You don't need to be an expert in your niche before you start, far from it people are eager to see what you have to share with them.

Even if you are not tech-savvy or have any technical experience, this book provides a detailed guide on how to start from scratch. Learn the secrets of the trade that will fast track your blog set up, build your audience and monetize it. The reason most bloggers don't turn a profit and naturally die is because they don't have a clear cut strategy on how to use the content they will be creating to sell their products or services. And this stems from not understanding their potential customer and the problem they are looking to solve. It is in understanding the problem your potential customer is trying to solve that you will be able to craft contents that offer valuable solutions and in turn make your blog profitable.

Writing a killer content that drives sales starts with creating your customer's avatar - what does he or she loves, his or her age, daily activities, and other things which might be as minute as the type of spectacle he or she wears, lol. Though funny but the smallest amount of detail is important in creating the avatar, because your blog will be about connecting with the avatar, making him or her understand that you understand his or her problems and provide a solution that he or she can't resist.

Your blog should be the gateway to your money-making marketing system. It is the first port of call for potential customers and I'll show you firsthand how to categorize your buyers to better serve them and make money doing so.

What are some of the results you'll expect?

1. Setting up your blog within a few minutes.

Many make the mistake of thinking that building a blog requires a high level of expertise and even give up before starting. In this book we are going to unpack the best and most secure way of setting up a blog with WordPress.

Show you the right plugins that will turn your blog to a performance monster without slowing down your website. Don't know what a plugin is? Don't worry, I explained it in the next chapters.

2. Build a raving audience

I will show you how to attract, nurture and convert your readers. And not only that, engage them with after sales value that will make them a raving fan of your blog.

Understand how to structure content that will speak directly to the readers' problem, make the reader see you as an authority in your niche, and won't be hesitant buying your offer.

3. Best monetization techniques

Many people make the mistake of posting random topics especially trending ones on their blogs with the hope they will monetize it with Google Ads.

While Google Ads is one of the monetization techniques, it is neither the only one nor the most lucrative. I will show you the best techniques to monetize your blog and how to align your content topics to promote sales.

Understand the 4 main stages of marketing

- **Attract**: Bringing the traffic to your blog using content
- **Capture**: Getting the readers to sign up to your mailing list
- **Engage**: Using your blog content to engage with your audience and subscribers to your mailing list. This is where you offer the reader tons of value to increase your mindshare and level of authority amongst your audience.
- **Convert**: If the 3 steps above are done well, this final Convert stage will be much easier. After all, by now, the reader you attracted with your beautiful content had handed over his email to you through the email opt-in plugin on your blog, read a bunch of your valuable blogs because you notified him via email as

soon as you published it and now ready to buy from you because he trusted you as an authority in your chosen niche.

4. Have a winning psychology

Blogging can be tough especially at the beginning. You need to have the right mental attitude to succeed when the going gets tough, when the traffic to your site is still low despite churning out excellent content. No need to be discouraged and throw in the towel, it is a matter of sitting down and analyzing what might be the cause of low traffic.

I will introduce you to my winning formula of using the power of dreams to keep my content wheel oiled up and grinding till the tide turns for good.

Now let's get to it.

DOWNLOAD YOUR BONUS PACK AT

https://tovalezeani.com/make-money-blogging-on-wordpress-bonus-pack/[2]

What's included in the bonus pack:

- 30+ actionable blog traffic generation sources that will jumpstart your traffic.
- 13 steps to implement military-grade security for your blog.
- 10+ productivity tools to make your work easier.
- 40+ free stock photo sites and 12 sites for free product mockups to enable you to create amazing blog posts and highly converting lead magnets.
- 15+ blog promotion tips for continuous sustainable growth.
- 60+ affiliate programs in 7 niches to get you started with the monetization of your blog.
- 6 best affiliate networks for beginners.

SECTION 1 - SETTING UP YOUR BLOG

1

NICHE SELECTION

Experts will always tell you to blog about your passion, although this is great advice, it is not enough. Finding a profitable niche is one of the vital elements of building a profitable blog.

Selecting the right niche is a critical factor in building a blog that is often overlooked. If you pick a niche with lots of competition, your blog will be beaten down by high authority websites giving you no chance to compete. On the other hand, if you pick a smaller niche with no demand, your blog will not have the needed eyeballs you can use to monetize it. You need to find a niche that's in the middle to low competition range and a good amount of audience.

In this chapter, I will show you how to spot those niches that have low competition and good amount of audience with the following practical steps

1. PICK A NICHE YOU ENJOY TALKING ABOUT OR READING ABOUT.

It's always enjoyable and fun setting up your blog, buying domain name, putting the finishing touches on your blog, and publishing the first article. But most bloggers lose interest and give up just a few months after starting because of traffic not pouring in as they would have wanted.

So, it's important that you pick a niche that you also like to learn and talk about. One that you will still love to write about a year, two or three years on.

Your niche could be about a hobby, area of expertise, or your exercise workout style (if you're into health and fitness). You don't have to be an expert on this topic. It just has to be a topic that gets you excited when talking about it and you're knowledgeable about it.

How do you pick a niche you're passionate about? Here's a quick test to figure that out. Take a pen and paper. Write down 20 things just off the top of your head that you enjoy or people consult you for. This exercise should help you quickly identify various niches you are passionate about. Now let's move to audience research to see which of the niches have a big enough audience.

2. DO AUDIENCE RESEARCH.

The logical next step is to make sure that there's a profitable and big enough market for your topic. This can be done with a small market research. Here's how you can get started.

For example, let's say that sewing is one of your favorite hobbies, and you want to start a blog about it. You need to do some data crunching to ascertain with laser pinpoint accuracy how viable the sewing niche would be.

It's always good to start your research with Google, the dominant search engine.

Google has an interesting free tool called *Google Trends* that enables you to take a sneak peek into their Big Data. As the name implies, this tool enables you to see Google trending searches.

Simply put your niche and hit search. It will display the public's interest in the niche keyword over a period ranging from an hour ago to more than fifteen years back.

Continuing with our sewing niche, you can see below that it has a fair stable amount of interest from the public for the past twelve months globally. This is a very good indication since we are only interested in niches that have ascending or high stable interest, meaning you'll have a big-enough audience to drive traffic to your blog for many years ahead. You don't want to start a blog in a niche with descending public interest.

Should you want to target a specific country, you can filter the result by country.

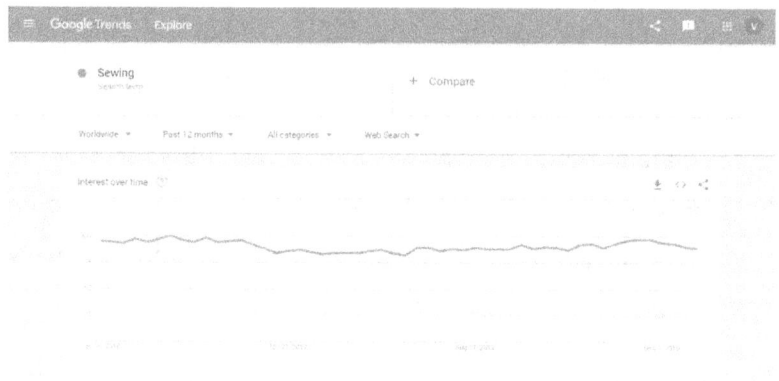

Google Trends - Courtesy Google

Then the next step, head to Google Keyword Planner[3]. This is a free tool within Google Ads. Here you want to look for a niche keyword that has high average monthly searches with low competition. This means that we need a niche that has moderate to high public interest/searches with low competition so we can be able to rank well on Google and draw traffic to our site. I normally recommend 10K-100K average monthly searches as the ideal number because it shows a sizable interest, and with good search engine optimization, you can easily rank on the first page of Google and be enjoying tons of organic traffic (eyeballs!) to your blog.

However, sometimes you might find that your chosen niche (in our case sewing)has a higher amount of average monthly searches (100K-1M) with low competition like below. This is equally good since it shows a larger audience with low competition.

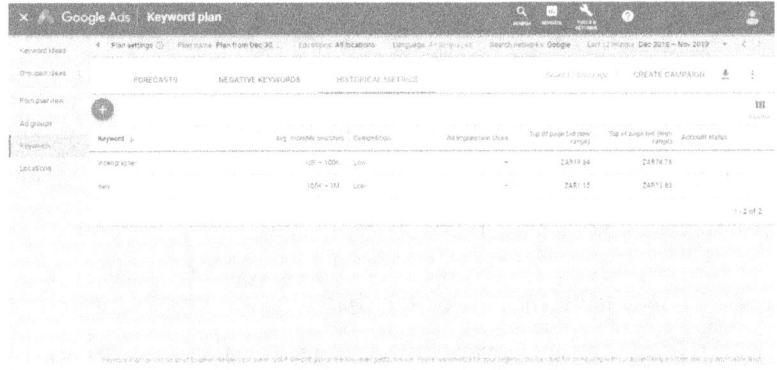

Google Ads - Courtesy Google.

3. PICK A SMALLER NICHE.

After audience research, the next thing is to narrow down on your chosen target audience or niche.

You can do this using smart tools like Ahrefs[4] and Semrush[5]. Both tools allow you to do an in-depth topic research of your niche.

Let's assume you want to blog about dogs, it's pretty obvious that dog niche is a very broad niche. There's dog training, dog food, dog treats, dog health, dog behavior, there's a ton to talk about in this niche!

You need to find your zone of genius in the dog sub-niches where your expertise is very strong and blog about it.

Picking a smaller niche lowers the competition and allows you to use your expertise to dominate the competition.

4. MAKE SURE IT'S PROFITABLE.

If you're planning on earning money from your blog, then you should make sure that your niche is profitable enough to enable you to earn a good income from your blog.

An easy way to test this is to see if any brands or businesses are advertising for your keywords. If people are spending money on AdWords to advertise products targeting specific keywords related to your niche, then you've picked the right topic.

This means you can easily monetize your blog with AdSense ads. However, a better and more profitable approach would be to promote affiliate products on your blog.

You can easily join Amazon's affiliate program to promote its products. Whenever you send a buying customer to Amazon, you'll earn a certain percentage as commission on each product they buy.

You can write a review post for example about rock climbing gears while using your affiliate links to direct traffic to the Amazon page where the gears are listed.

ACTION STEPS

Go ahead and list topics you love, follow the above steps you have learned to sieve out a niche that has a good interest with low competition. Now proceed to the next chapter where we'll make use of our niche topic to coin a domain name and choose our web hosting service provider.

2

WEB HOSTING

Now it is the time to host your blog on the internet with a web hosting company. But before that, you need to choose a domain name for your blog. A domain name can simply be seen as your brand name. It is the name that people will enter on their browser to get to your blog.

There are various domain registrars on the web and all web hosting companies provide domain registration, however, I always prefer to register my domain with *namecheap.com* not only because of their cheap domain prices but also the high availability of various Top Level Domain (TLD) to choose from other than *.com*. Other TLD available are .tips, .red, .co, .io etc

DOMAIN SEARCH AND REGISTRATION

From our niche research in the last chapter, we'll have to coin a name that will achieve these two objectives:

- **Same as your focus keyword** - Focus keyword is simply your niche related word of which you will like to rank for on Google. Making your focus keyword your domain name helps in ranking higher on Google because of some algorithmic weightings that Google gives on domains that match or are related to a search query. For example, let's say our focus keywords are *embroidery machine* we can choose embroiderymachine.com. Most times the .com TLD is not available for our chosen keyword, this is where various TLD that Namecheap offers comes handy. You can choose *.net, .co, .io, .tips* etc. I chose *.tips* when registering my blog *passiveincome.tips* because my focus keyword is passive income and passiveincome.com is not available. Some people think that Google ranks *.com* TLD higher than other TLDs but my experience registering and scaling a none *.com* TLD website confirms that Google treats all TLDs the same.
- **Easy to remember** - Make sure that your domain name is easy to remember and doesn't contain a hyphen (-). People are too busy nowadays with so

many things begging for their attention. So a domain name that is concise and easy to remember will help to engrave your blog in the minds of your audience.

It is also important to ensure that your domain registrar offers domain privacy. This feature shields your registration details from spammers and I recommend you click the domain privacy whilst registering a domain.

With domain registration done, let's now proceed to important factors to consider when choosing a web host.

Uptime and Server Reliability

Weak and unstable servers provide unstable network connections that will often put your site offline. It should be avoided at all costs. You can't work so hard to bring traffic to your site, only for readers to visit your site and have the bad experience of it being offline. Choosing a hosting company with reputable uptime scores, preferably above 99.9 percent is, therefore, key to your site's success. Avoid companies that report an annual uptime score below 99 percent.

Customer Service

Customer service support should be on your top list. Companies that offer only email support no longer cut it these days, choose a host that offers live chat support as well as social media presence. Web hosting companies with in-house customer support departments should be given priority as opposed to web hosting companies that outsourced theirs, since the in-house support department always has a better understanding of the hosting service than the outsourced team.

User Friendliness of Control Panel

Good and user-friendly control panel is quite important so you don't waste a lot of time trying to figure out the simplest task like the creation of email. Also, the control panel must have a WordPress Quick installation feature to automate your WordPress installation and save you a ton of time. Cpanel and Plesk are the best control panels in the market currently and most web hosting companies use it.

Unlimited Websites

Some hosting companies don't support hosting unlimited websites with just one hosting account so you need to ensure that your hosting company supports it. *Hosting unlimited websites* on a single account is a must-have feature because you might need to expand your offering in the future with a brand new website that you can host with your already existing hosting account. This helps to keep all your websites under one hosting account as an example, you can have *embroidery-sewing.com* and *embroiderydesigns.com* both on the same hosting account eliminating the need to buy a hosting account every time you need to launch a new website.

Storage Type and Space

Unlimited storage space is common now amongst hosting companies but you need to make sure that the hard drive is Solid State Drive (SSD) and not a mechanical hard drive. Solid State hard drive is faster than a mechanical hard drive and will contribute to the fastness of your site. When looking out for this feature, try to ascertain if the host is using SSD for everything or only for their key applications. To fully benefit from the speed of SSDs, your web files also need to reside on the SSD.

Parked Domains

You need to find out if you can easily park your company's other domain names. This might not be a service that you need at the beginning but as you become successful you may need to buy hyphenated versions of your domain name, misspellings, service names, and more. It's most efficient and convenient for brand management to have these in one control panel and know that you're not going to lose any traffic to a competitor.

Backup and Recovery

This is another crucial factor to put into consideration because you won't want to lose all your content in case of any mishap. Find out from the hosting company's support how their backup and recovery works. Anything IT-related is open to possible failure and having a backup could mean the difference between a quick recovery and total loss.

Backup systems can be manual or automated. Doing it manually requires that you perform the backup yourself, or at the very least must initiate the start of the backup operation. Automated systems are more convenient and can be set up to perform backups at set intervals.

Spam Prevention System

Some web hosting companies go the extra mile to set up a spam prevention system that offers that extra layer of security for your website. This type of system uses artificial intelligence to detect and prevent abnormal malicious intrusions into their network.

Working with a web hosting company that understands cyber-security and always stays a step ahead of hackers is non-negotiable. I love how Bluehost.com tackled this with dedicated spam experts.

Scalability

While you might be starting with a smaller hosting package now, think long term and partner with a hosting company that can take care of your traffic as you grow. This means that the company should offer different tiers of service based on the number of expected visitors you receive each month where, as your business takes off, you can easily upgrade your plan. Just as importantly, you may want to evaluate providers based on how they deal with unexpected spikes in bandwidth. Additionally, you need to make sure that spikes don't cost you an arm and a leg as some providers charge you very ridiculous amounts of money for additional usage.

Easy to Install SSL Certificate

Secure Sockets Layer (SSL) is a standard security technology for establishing an encrypted link between a server and a client—typically a web server (website) and a browser, or a mail server and a mail client (e.g., Gmail).

You need to understand that search engines in a bid to promote safe browsing love sites that have Secured Socket Layer certificates. SSL certificates help assure users that the website they are visiting is safe, which is crucial for peace of mind. They are especially vital for websites that store or process user information or process financial information such as on e-commerce websites. The key thing here is to check and see if your web hosting plan will support an SSL certificate and how easy it is to install it from the control panel. As shown below the red marked padlock signifies that the site has an SSL certificate.

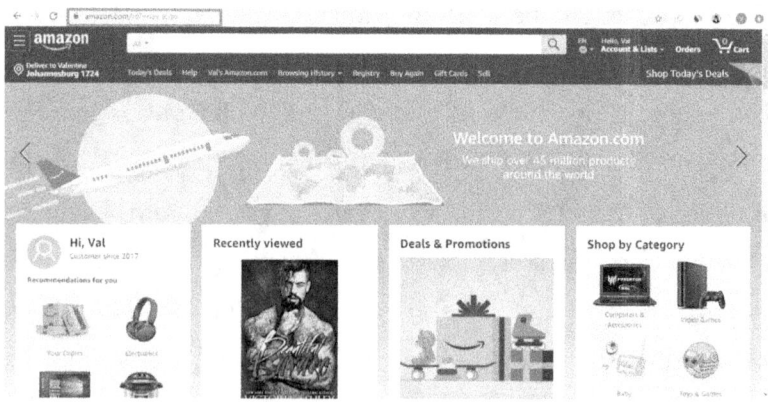

Amazon - Courtesy Amazon.

ACTION STEPS

Considering all the factors above, it is now time to select your web hosting company. Having satisfied all the conditions above I recommend the *Choice Plus* Package of Bluehost[6] web hosting company. It is a complete package and all you need to get started. Click here[7] to get it.

3
WORDPRESS AND THEME INSTALLATIONS

Now you've chosen your service provider based on the factors above. The next step is to set up WordPress and install your theme.

Upon payment, the web hosting company will send you a simple to follow email guide to access your control panel. Use the default password to access the control panel and immediately change your password. I will show you how to install WordPress on Bluehost the quick way and for those that are tech-savvy and may prefer the FTP (File Transfer Protocol) method, the steps are also explained below.

QUICK WORDPRESS INSTALLATION

I recommended Bluehost because they provide excellent hosting service and they know WordPress inside out and have the most beginner-friendly WordPress installation process.

Bluehost automatically installs WordPress on your domain name when you sign up. Follow the below steps to install WordPress on your Bluehost web hosting account.

Step 1: Log in to Bluehost

Once you login to your Bluehost account, click on 'My Sites' tab

Step 2: Enter your website information

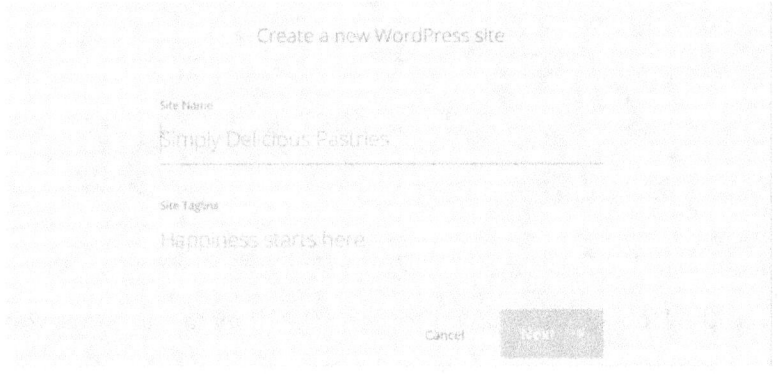

Next, you need to enter some basic information about your

website, including the Site Name and Site Tagline. Remember you can always change these later.

Except for their 'Basic' plan, Bluehost also allows you to install WordPress on unlimited sites with all their hosting plans. As I said earlier this is important because in future you might need to expand your brand by launching more sites related to your niche.

Step 3: Choose your domain name

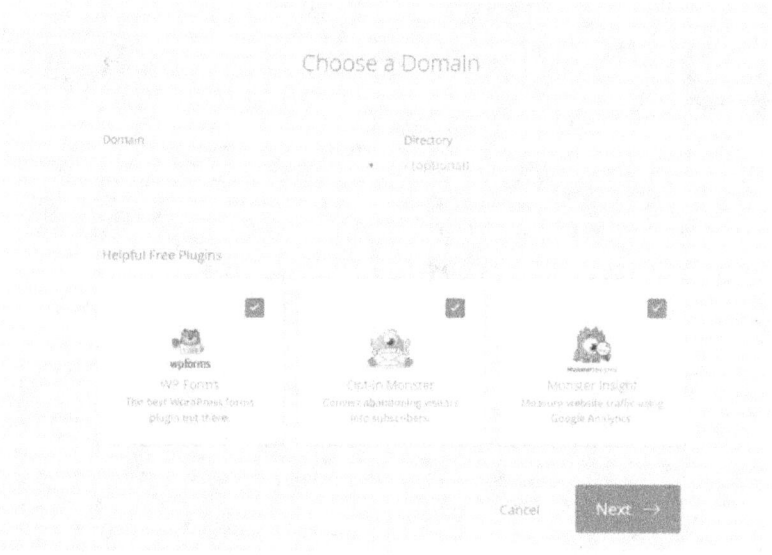

Use the Domain drop-down to select the domain name that you chose when you created your Bluehost account. You can also choose whether or not to install some of Bluehost's recommended plugins. I will discuss more about plugins in the next chapter.

Step 4: Click "Next" to install WordPress on Bluehost

Bluehost will now install WordPress for you, creating your new WordPress website, and displaying your login details.

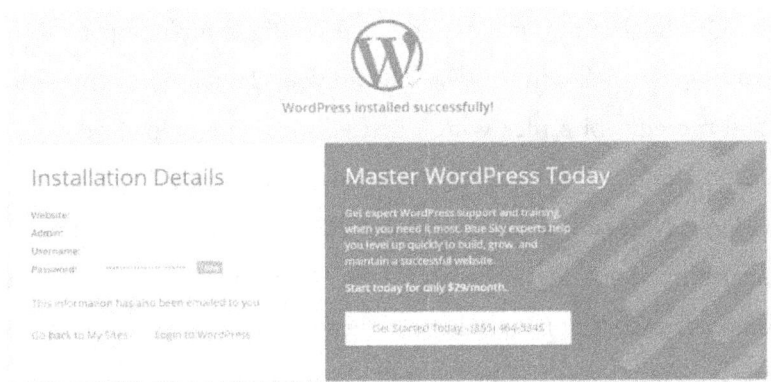

You will also receive these details via email. You can now click on the login to WordPress button to enter your new site's admin area.

That's all. Easy right?

FTP WORDPRESS INSTALLATION (OPTIONAL)

For the tech-savvy, this method entails downloading the latest version of WordPress from https://wordpress.org/download/[8] and following the steps below

1. Download and unzip the WordPress package if you haven't already.

2. Create a database for WordPress on your web server, as well as a MySQL user who has all privileges for accessing and modifying it. You can jump to *Create the Database and a User* before continuing.

3. (Optional) Find and rename wp-config-sample.php to wp-config.php, then edit the file and add your database information. You can edit .php files with a text editor like Notepad or a tool called Notepad++. I use the Notepad++ for my editing. You can Google Notepad++ to download the latest version, it's free. I recommend you leave this step 3 for WordPress to do it for you automatically upon installation, just get the following details ready because you will be prompted for it.

- DB_NAME *(The name of the database you created, more on database creation below)*
- DB_USER *(The database username)*
- DB_PASSWORD *(The password you chose for the database)*
- DB_HOST *(Usually localhost will suffice)*
- DB_CHARSET *(normally should not be changed).*
- DB_COLLATE *(The database collation should normally be left blank)*

4. Once again: If you are not comfortable with renaming files,

step 3 is optional. You can skip it for WordPress to do it for you.

5. Upload the WordPress files to the desired location on your web server:

If you want to integrate WordPress into the root of your domain (e.g. http://yoursite.com/), move or upload all contents of the unzipped WordPress directory (excluding the WordPress directory itself) into the root directory of your web server most times */Public_html* folder

If you want to have your WordPress installation in its own subdirectory on your website (e.g. http://yoursite.com/blog/), create the blog directory on your server and upload the contents of the unzipped WordPress package to the directory (*/public_html/blog*) via FTP.

Note: I use a free FTP client called FileZilla for uploading the unzipped WordPress contents to the */Public_html* web server folder. You can download it at https://filezilla-project.org/[9]

6. Run the WordPress installation script by accessing your site URL in a web browser. This should be the URL where you uploaded the WordPress files.

7. If you installed WordPress in the root directory, you should visit: http://yoursite.com/

8. If you installed WordPress in its own subdirectory called blog, for example, you should visit: http://yoursite.com/blog/

That's it! Your WordPress should now be installed.

WORDPRESS THEMES

WordPress themes are pre-built templates and stylesheets you can install to define your site appearance.

WordPress comes with its themes that can be installed and used straight out of the box. However, I recommend you use premium themes for that professional look your site deserves.

You can get premium themes from sites like *themeforest.net* and *templatemonster.com*. There are a host of others but I prefer those two. I love themes because they make your website development very easy. Simply search for the category of themes you need (in our case search 'blog themes' and if you are building an e-commerce store search 'e-commerce themes') then filter results by WordPress themes to show you only WordPress themes. Then select the one you like, pay, and download it.

WordPress Theme Installation

The theme file is usually downloaded in .zip format (compressed file), don't bother extracting it, simply go sign in to your WordPress dashboard and click on Appearance > Themes > Add new to upload your new theme.

WordPress will automatically extract the contents and install the theme for you. Upon completion just click activate to make the newly installed theme your primary theme.

After the theme installation, you can start customizing it according to your needs. Most themes provide a detailed *How-To* video guide and email support to help with this.

Remember that your theme is changeable, You can always get a new theme at any time, follow the same process, and activate it. Always go for themes that have in-built social share buttons and Email opt-in to avoid using a plugin to add this functionality.

ACTION STEPS

Now that you have learned about WordPress installations and theme activation it's time to head to Bluehost[10] and sign up for a hosting package, follow the processes explained in *Quick WordPress Installation* above to install your WordPress then get your premium theme, install and activate it.

Congratulations, you now have a brand new blog ready to share with the world. In the next chapter, we will dive straight into blog security and enhancement using plugins. Let's get to it.

4

SECURING AND ENHANCING YOUR BLOG WITH PLUGINS

P lugin is a piece of software you install on your WordPress to extend the functionality or add new features. Numerous plugins do various functions, you can discover them on the WordPress dashboard under Appearance.

INSTALLING SECURE SECURITY LAYER (SSL) CERTIFICATE

Securing your blog starts with the installation of an SSL certificate from your Cpanel.

To enable the free SSL certificate:

1. Log into your Bluehost control panel.
2. Click the My Sites tab from the side navigation menu to the left.

SECURING AND ENHANCING YOUR BLOG WITH PLUGI... | 37

3. Locate the site you wish to activate the free SSL for and click the manage button.
4. Open the Security tab.
5. Under Security Certificate toggle the Free SSL ON.

After successful activation, you will start seeing the padlock sign before your URL on the browser address tab. Also your URL now starts with https:// and no longer http://

How to Install Plugin

Having finished the installation of SSL, let's now move on with plugin installation. This is a pretty easy exercise, login to your WordPress dashboard and click Plugins > Add plugins, then search for the plugin you want to install and click *Install Now* after which you activate it.

9 RECOMMENDED PLUGINS

As I said before there are plenty of plugins out there that aim to enhance and improve your blog functionality, but these nine are 'must-have' plugins.

Premium Site Theme

1. Divi

Anti Spam & Security

2. Limit Login Attempts Reloaded

3. Akismet Anti-Spam

Site Monitoring

4. Google Analytics Dashboard for WP (GADWP)

On-Page SEO

5. Rank Math SEO

6. Smush - For image compression

7. W3 Total Cache

Back & Restore

8. UpdraftPlus - Backup/Restore

Content Publishing

9. WordPress Editorial Calendar

ACTION STEPS

Head over to your WordPress dashboard and install these plugins for optimal blog performance.

5

BASIC SEO: HOW TO RANK HIGHER ON GOOGLE

No one likes to perform for an empty audience. That is how I see a blog without traffic. You won't like to spend your time researching and writing amazing blog posts and no one is reading. It will be a wasted effort.

Hence Search Engine Optimization (SEO) is crucial for your blog to rank well on Google and bring you tons of traffic. As I'm going to explain in the next chapter, traffic are leads or potential customers which you are going to capture to start the sales process. More on that in the next chapter.

For now, let's look at making our blog Google friendly. SEO is divided into three major categories: On-page, Technical and Off-page SEOs.

I will explain to you in this chapter about these three major categories so you can consciously inculcate the best practices into your blog from day one.

ON-PAGE SEO

On-page SEO is all about the content on your website.

It is the process of optimizing individual site pages to rank better for your primary target keywords and drive relevant traffic. Primary target keywords being the relevant word or phrase you want your blog post to rank for on Google.

While On-page SEO is about optimizing every single page of your blog, it needs to be supported by both Technical and Off-page SEO. On-page SEO alone may not be enough to get a page to rank. You also need an Off-page and Technical SEO to help your overall site rank in major search engines.

The following 15-point On-Page SEO checklist should guide every blog post you publish to draw relevant traffic.

1. Perform Keyword Research

Your On-page SEO should start with keyword research. Which keyword do you want to target and rank for? Because of stiff competition, it is always good to go for long-tail keywords. They are keywords with longer word counts generally 3 to 4 or more words. There are numerous software tools for doing this research however my best tool is Semrush[11]. I always use it for my keyword research.

The best keyword is the phrase or term that satisfies the below:

- It is relevant to the main topic or theme of the content.
- It is regularly searched for by your target audience. The search volume for the keyword is large enough to drive traffic to your site from your ideal target audience.
- Is within your site's competitive power. Your domain has enough authority to rank above other sites already ranking for that keyword. In simple terms, Domain Authority is a measure of a site's authority and relevance for a specific subject area. It is measured on a scale of 1-100 with 0 being the lowest score and 100 highest score.

2. Choose one primary keyword for each blog post.

As soon as you choose your keyword, assign it to one blog post on your site. Create an editorial calendar for new blog posts and assign a target keyword to each post. Don't assign a keyword to more than one post to avoid keyword cannibalization issues. wherein search engines don't know which post is more important and, therefore, rank neither post.

3. Include your keyword in your content title.

Your title should be appealing to both search engines and your audience. Write catchy titles with your primary keyword at the beginning of the title. It should be descriptive and concise enough for your audience to understand what the content is all about at a glance. Rank Math SEO plugin will guide on this as you start writing your content, it will be giving you SEO tips to follow to properly optimize your content, action those tips.

4. Put your title in an H1 tag.

Always wrap the title in an H1 title tag. An H1 title tag is a piece of HTML code that tells search engines that the copy is the title of the page and an important description of the content.

5. Write more than 500 words of body content.

The number of words for your content will vary depending on the page's purpose and the depth of the topic. Search engines like indexing and ranking longer form articles, so do aim for at least 1500+ words when possible, as more detailed posts will have a higher probability of ranking.

6. Create a primary keyword density of 2-3% keyword density.

Assist search engines to recognize the main theme of your content by using the primary keyword throughout the copy. As a best practice, use the term two to three times per 100 words to create a 2-3% keyword density. Try not to go over this limit to avoid keyword stuffing issues.

7. Write scannable content.

Both readers and search engines like content that is easy to scan and understand. Go through your content and use formatting that makes it easy to quickly scan and review.

- Break contents into sections with descriptive subheadings.
- Use bullet points for lists of information.
- Use bold formatting or callouts to highlight important points.

8. Write subheadings in an H2 tag.

Teach search engines to identify the subheadings in your content (and the main points of your copy) by putting the phrases in an H2 tag. Like the H1 tag used on your headline, this HTML code tells search engines that the copy is important and related to the primary page topic.

9. Include relevant internal links using targeted anchor text.

Links help search engines connect and understand online content. Refer and link to relevant internal pages while writing your content, and when possible use the linked page's target keyword as the anchor text for the link.

10. Add relevant links to high-quality sites.

Outgoing links to other sites also add context that helps search crawlers understand your content. So also include relevant, valuable, and high-quality outbound links that lead to other pages when you mention a resource or cite a source within your content.

11. Include at least one image.

The click-through rate of any content with an image is always higher than one without. The image makes the content captivating and draws the reader's attention to read the content. Ensure all your contents have relevant images on it and always compress the image with WP Smush plugin to reduce the file size and use your keyword on the image's Alt tag.

12. Write an SEO-friendly URL that includes the primary keyword.

WordPress shows you the URL of each page with an editing option. Because of ranking weightings that search engines put on URL, ensure that your page URL includes the primary keyword. Avoid adding any stop words, special characters, or unnecessary words in the permalink.

13. Assign relevant tags and categories.

Blog's tags and categories help to organize content and guide search engines in understanding topics. If you publish a blog post, add categories and tags that are relevant to the theme of the content.

14. Add an optimized meta description.

A meta description is a brief information that supports the title. It also helps search engines understand the content and is displayed on SERP (Search Engine Result Pages). Add an optimized meta description that has fewer than 320 characters, includes the primary keyword near the front of the description, and includes a soft call to action encouraging readers to click

15. Proofread your content.

You need to go through your work before you publish it. Proofread the content for spelling and grammatical errors. This is an essential part of writing, as it ensures your content is high-quality, authoritative, and worthy of being displayed on Google's first-page search result.

TECHNICAL SEO

Technical SEO is about non-content elements of your website.

It includes strategies and actions to improve a site's backend structure and foundation. Technical SEO improves a site's readability (which makes it easy for search engines to crawl and understand the site) and provides a good user experience, which helps search engines see that the site is high quality. A good user experience is also important for readers and can affect overall traffic and engagement rates.

The types of SEO included in this category relate to:

- Site speed
- Mobile-friendliness
- Indexing
- Crawlability
- Site architecture
- Structured data
- Security

An easy way to check on the state of your technical SEO is by using Google Search Console. Once you have connected your site, it shows you the above data insights about your site along with instructions on how to resolve any issue that is detected on your site. You can get it here[12].

OFF-SITE SEO

Off-page SEO deals with techniques that help strengthen the influence and relationship your website has with other websites.

It includes strategies to build a website's reputation and authority. These are the things that help search engines see that a website is an ideal search result because it is from a reputable, reliable, trusted source.

Most off-site SEO relates to building high-quality backlinks. A large volume of links pointing to your site from relevant, authoritative sites shows search engines that your site is valuable and established, thus making the search engine to rank it high.

You can build these trust signals through a variety of link building and guest posting tactics.

Start your link building plan by analyzing your competitor's Backlink using Semrush. Analyze up to 10 competitor sites, download the report, and to gain ideas on how you can build links to the same sites.

ACTION STEPS

Use this chapter as a guide whenever you are writing your blog posts and don't do comprehensive keyword and competitor's research without Semrush[13].

SECTION 2 - BUILD YOUR TRIBE

6

CONTENT STRATEGY THAT FUELS SALES

The soul of every blog is the quality of its content. According to Content Marketing Institute[14] *2020 B2B Content Marketing Research Report,* there has been a year on year growth in the success rate of organizations with a documented content marketing strategy with 2020 recording the highest rate of 69%.

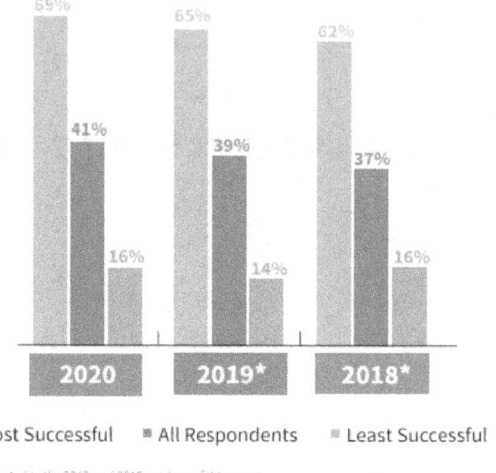

Courtesy - Content Marketing Institute.

Quality content is also an important ranking factor for search engines. Writing a quality content (one that fuels sales) starts with a content strategy, a clear cut plan that takes into cognizance the following key points which we are going to deal with in this chapter.

- Setting a goal - Your offer.
- Understanding the purchase readiness of the target reader.
- How to get into the buyer's mind.

- How to use an old key copywriting style that still converts.
- Embedding a strong call to action.

SETTING A GOAL - YOUR OFFER

Your content strategy should start with setting a goal for the blog post. What exactly do you want the blog to achieve? Generation of leads? Brand awareness? Educate prospects and customers on what to do? Or generate sales?

Be as specific as possible with your goal, being generic like saying "generating more sales" is not good enough. Instead aim to achieve specific targets like "increasing my sales by 15%". Having a clearly defined goal will set you up to push through all the other steps, all the hours of writing, and all the obstacles bound to show up without relenting or losing focus.

Remember you're not in competition with anyone else to produce more content but you're competing to win the eyeballs of the readers. The money is in the eyeballs, the more eyeballs you can get to your blog the more money you make. With this in mind, you need to craft your content around your offer with a catchy title that begs click me. One of the reasons most bloggers don't turn a profit is because they are just churning out what I like to call 'Offer-less" content. Contents that are not written to promote a specific offer.

All your blog posts must have a goal around which the blog content will be built.

READER'S AWARENESS LEVEL

Like I have said earlier, before you start writing your blog post you need to know who the content is meant for, what you will be offering, and thirdly the reader's or prospect's level of awareness.

Eugene Schwartz tackled this issue in his classic book **Breakthrough Advertising** back in 1966.

Schwartz broke down prospect awareness into five distinct phases:

Completely Unaware: Prospects who have no idea a problem or solution to exits. They are the coldest of cold prospects.

Problem-Aware: Your prospect senses he has a problem, and is now researching for a solution.

Solution-Aware: Your prospect knows the result he wants, but not sure that your product provides it.

Product-Aware: Your prospect knows what you sell, but isn't sure it's right for him

The Most Aware: Your prospect knows your product, and only needs to know "the deal."

Let's now take a closer look at each stage and how we can use it to craft content that has high chances of conversion.

COMPLETELY UNAWARE

These are prospects who have no clue what their problem or solution is. They most probably haven't heard about your blog. They are prospects I like to call "passers-by". Most often they stumble upon your blog through social media or search engines.

Content Strategy: The Completely Unaware is the most difficult of the prospects and the largest. This difficulty stems from their problem unawareness, since one needs to acknowledge a problem first before seeking a solution. Contents for these prospects are mostly educative contents that highlights problems and solutions. Assuming you are in the golf niche, a content example will be writing a blog that explains the correlation of back pain and playing golf which most golf beginners don't know about.

PROBLEM AWARE

These prospects are aware of their problem and are now researching for a solution. Most people turn to Google for answers when they identify their problem and want a solution.

A well-researched keyword is important at this stage for good ranking on search engines. Also question and answer forums are one of the best places to get these kinds of prospects and lead them through your sales funnel.

Content Strategy: This is where your blogging can be most potent. Create a blog post that resonates with the prospect, showing that you truly understand his problem and how your offer is the solution.

SOLUTION AWARE

This stage goes hand in hand with the Problem Aware stage. Your blog should aim to walk through the problem recognition phase to a solution aware stage. And while you are providing all these valuable contents to the prospect within the various stages, you're gradually building trust in the mind of the prospect which will make closing a deal natural.

Content Strategy: The prospect here kind of knows what the solution to his problem will look like but might not yet be sure. Hence write contents that explain the problem and pitch your offer as a solution. Most importantly give more detail why your offer is better because the prospect at this stage hasn't decided yet on the particular solution to buy but he is getting ready.

PRODUCT AWARE

A reader in this stage is someone who has identified his or her problem, knows that a solution exists but isn't yet sure that your offer is the right choice.

Content Strategy: This type of reader is still shopping around for the right solution but his card is itching in his pocket. What you need to do to get his dollar is creating a laser-focused content that addresses his or her problem and why your offer is best suited for the problem. For example a blog like this: *10 reasons why Shopify is better than Woocommerce* can be used to target someone who wants to start an e-commerce store that is at this stage.

THE MOST AWARE

These are readers that are fully aware of their problem or pain point that needs to be solved and also know how your offer will help them solve this problem. They are the most ripe or ready to buy readers of your content.

Content Strategy: Craft contents that address a specific pain point of theirs and pitch your offer within the content. For example if you're an online Digital Marketing Agency you can craft content that targets e-commerce shop owners with a blog like this - *How to generate more sales within 24 hours.* You can notice that I used 24 hours in the title because it creates a time frame and sense of urgency in the mind of the reader and it also boosts clicks. In the blog you then explain how your agency can assist the shop owner to generate sales within 24 hours by generating leads from various online media sources and then subtly pitch your marketing package.

CRAFT YOUR CONTENT

Having identified the awareness level of your prospect, the next thing is to get into the minds of your prospect. For a few moments, try and think like your prospect. I normally like to focus on *Product Aware* and *The Most Aware* group of prospects. I try to figure out what keywords they are most likely to be typing on Google and I'll use those keywords as my content key focus keywords

Before writing any blog, you must understand your target's behavioral patterns- how they think, talk and even going as far as knowing the language they use and respond to. What are their fears and frustrations? What gets them excited and motivated? Knowing all these allows you to craft a laser targeted blog post that will convert.

You know about all these retail by doing background research on the target audience before writing your blog post.

You need to understand that people buy with emotion first and then justify it with logic afterward. Tap into this weakness by crafting an emotionally appealing content. Content that leverages at least one of the five major motivators of human behavior, especially buying:

1. Fear
2. Love
3. Greed
4. Guilt
5. Pride

Blog titles are one of the most important parts of your blog. It must be catchy enough to do its job of grabbing the attention of the reader and get them to click and start reading. See how some of these successful campaigns pushed one or more of the five major motivators of human behavior.

- Absolute Power Corrupts. Enjoy - Apple
- They don't write songs about Volvos - Chevrolet Corvette
- Picks up five times more women than a Lamborghini - Daihatsu
- I Love Herpes. Love is blind - Durex condom
- 525 horses working in a way that animal rights associations could complain about - Mercedes Benz
- Smoking reduces weight ... One lung at a time - Cancer Patients Aid Association

You get the drift now right?, Your blog is a business and treat it as such by using the same tactics of *emotional direct response copywriting* that Fortune 500 companies use.

ACTION STEPS

Always start each blog post by researching and targeting a specific segment of the Consumer Awareness Level.

CONTENT SEO OPTIMIZATION

Content SEO optimization deals with ways to structure your content so that it will be search engine friendly, ranking well for relevant people to see it.

It's not good to create content that nobody reads or knows about. An SEO optimized content is one that follows proven steps that works in ranking and that's what we'll be dealing with in this chapter, let's go straight into it.

TOPIC KEYWORD RESEARCH

If you have been following the guidelines of niche finding explained in Chapter 1, you should have defined your niche by now. Next is selecting a topic that is not only relevant but solves a particular problem for the targeted audience.

The selection of blog topics go hand in hand with keywords to target. Use smart tools like Google Keyword Planner and Semrush to research keywords properly. Not targeting your content to specific keywords from the start, will make you struggle to rank the blog post on Google.

Rank Math Seo WordPress Plugin is very good for optimizing your blog content to rank well. It not only shows you what needs to be done but offers tips on how to do them.

You need to determine for each content if it's a cornerstone content or supporting content. A cornerstone content is a pillar content of your site. It is the most important article of your site you want to rank highest in the search engine. Supporting contents as the name implies are contents that relate and link back to cornerstone content. A good blend of pillar and supporting articles improves your blog internal links and makes it easy for Google search engine algorithms to understand what your blog is all about and rank it properly.

I always recommend that you go for long-tail keywords. Long-tail keywords are more targeted and in marketing the better the targeting the better the conversion rate which is what you want. Also, long-tail keywords tend to have less competition than shorter keywords.

For example, if you're into men's fashion blogging, you can quickly spot a high volume keyword with very low keyword difficulty as shown below. Analyzing the keyword *1920s mens fashion* shows a low keyword difficulty of 12 and a high monthly search volume of 14 000. This shows a clear traffic opportunity for the keyword *1920s mens fashion*.

In case you don't know, keyword difficulty measures the level of difficulty to rank on Google's first page for a keyword. The difficulty is measured on a scale of 1- 100 with 1 being very easy and 100 most difficult.

The picture below shows the keyword (1920s mens fashion) analysis using Ahrefs.

Courtesy: Ahrefs.com

BLOG TITLE

With your target keyword selected, you'll now move to craft a perfect catchy title. Remember this is one of your best opportunities to attract the attention of a reader, so it needs your maximum creativity. Continuing with our selected keyword, a catchy blog title will be something like - 10 Easy 1920s Men's Fashion Ideas.

Another insightful tool for content SEO optimization is *buzzsumo.com*. It lets you know at a glance contents that perform well in your niche. You can use this knowledge of how top-performing blog titles are written to craft your blog title. Also from it you can equally see the social platforms a content is shared the most.

This is quite informative because it points to you where your likely audience spends most of their time so you can devote more time to the platform.

Your blog title should be all about attracting attention that leads to clicks. I normally use the following 4 major guides to write a blog post title.

1. Popular Headline Formula

If you pay attention to search results on Google, you'll notice that most titles follow this popular formula and there has been some research that found some clear trends in what people choose to click on.

A few types of headlines that routinely perform well include:

- *Number* headlines – Any headline that starts with a number, introducing a list post. E.g *10 Easy 1920s Men's Fashion Ideas.*

- *How to* headlines – This is a simple option, but a good one. If someone's trying to figure out how to do something, a headline that lets them know the blog post will solve their problem will attract clicks. E.g *How to Build Your Mailing List.*
- Famous comparison – Headlines like this borrow on the popularity of a person or piece of entertainment to get people to click. Depending on the famous thing or person you choose, they can add an element of fun to your blog, e.g. *Business Lessons I Learned from Watching Game of Thrones (but make sure the lesson is relevant to the show).*
- Scarcity headline – A headline that promises the reader something few people have. It normally starts with *"The Secret of..." or "Little Known Tips for..."* both titles are playing on this principle.
- Big promises headline – These headlines are assuring the reader that they'll be getting a lot of information if they click, this category includes headlines that start with *"The Ultimate Guide to..."* or *"Do ...3 times faster".*

Buzzsumo has also done extensive research into the words and phrases that perform best in headlines - mainly on Facebook. You don't need to just insert these words into your blog titles thoughtlessly, but if you keep them top of mind and look for opportunities to use them effectively, they could help you build better titles.

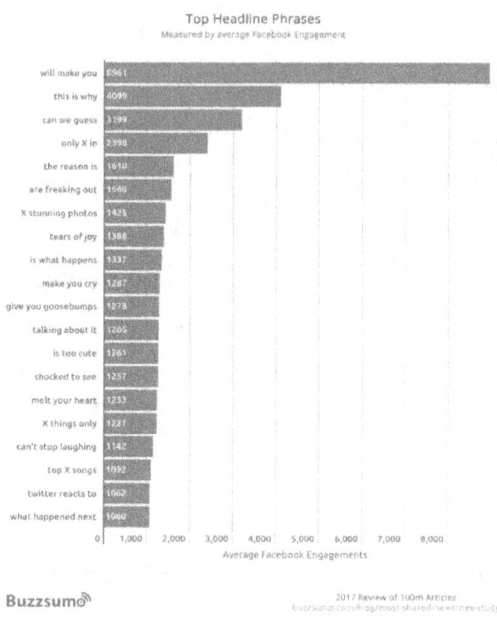

Courtesy: Buzzsumo.com

2. Arouse Curiosity

We are all curious animals. Tapping into this fundamental human behavior is another good strategy you can use to improve your headlines and blog post titles.

By doing so, you will make it difficult for the reader to leave without having first satisfied that curiosity by at least skimming your blog post. E.g using words like *"Find Out How.."*

3. Use Trigger/Power Words in your headlines

These are words or phrases that trigger a psychological response on the reader's part.

They are very useful, as they can compel people to take action and make decisions when an alternate choice of words would not.

The following is a sample list of some "trigger/power words" that you may want to use in your blog post titles or headlines:

> *Free*
> *News*
> *Shocking*
> *Introducing*
> *Announcing*
> *Proven*
> *Explosive*

4. Be Specific

Blog readers need a story they can visualize if you want them to take action. They have questions and they want answers, and if they can't visualize the solution that your headline or title suggests, then they won't bother to read further.

The more specific you can be the more your readers will appreciate it thus creating a long-lasting connection with them and building your authority in your niche.

Once you have come up with some blog title headlines, use

headline analyzer tools like Coschedule's headline analyzer tool[15] and AMI's tool[16] to test them and see which ones are most likely to perform well.

BLOG BODY

Once again, this is another place you will need the magic of Rank Math SEO plugin as it makes sure you incorporate all vital SEO ingredients in your content.

It will check and remind you to use H1 and H2 headings where necessary. H1 heading is simply an *HTML tag* that aids the search engine crawl bot to understand and appropriately rank your content while crawling the internet.

H1 helps the bot to understand that this is an important heading whilst the smaller sized H2 is mainly a subheading. Using H1 on main heading and H2 on subheadings also helps users to skim through your content and easily refer to sections they are most interested in.

Don't forget to remember that the search engine you want to bless you with traffic is not a human being, but an algorithm that needs your assistance to understand your content very well to rank it appropriately and serve your page to relevant audiences.

Write in plain English and keep paragraphs short. The longer, more complicated your sentences are, the more difficult it is to retain your readers' attention. Always keep it simple.

Use images on all posts. Contents with images are known to have attracted more attention and clicks than ones without images, so use them!

Sprinkling your main keyword throughout the body of the content to at least achieve some keyword density. Keyword density is the percentage of the number of times a keyword appears on a page divided by the total number of words on that page. For example, if in your article of 100 words you used your keyword 10 times, your density will be 10%. Although there is no ideal number, 10% might be too high.

Google suggests placing your keywords naturally in your content and doesn't like keyword stuffing. Rank Math SEO plugin guides and shows you a post's keyword density as you write.

Wrap up your content with a conclusion. Readers don't like contents that end abruptly. So be creative with your conclusion summary and finish off with some sort of call to action that will compel your readers to do what you want them to do, be it to join your mailing list or click your affiliate link or buy your offer.

ACTION STEPS

Hit that **Add New Post** button in your WordPress to start creating your first post putting into effect all you have learned in this chapter.

8

DRIVING TRAFFIC TO YOUR BLOG

After you have SEO optimized your content, it is now time to share it with the world. One of the major challenges that bloggers face, especially beginners, is how to drive traffic to their blogs.

The blogging space is highly competitive and spending hours writing content without someone to read it is very discouraging. But don't despair, in this chapter we are going to lay bare proven ways to get you right in front of your first readers. Let's get started.

RESEARCH YOUR AUDIENCE DIGITAL RENDEZVOUS

You need to research and know your *Audience Digital Rendezvous*. This is my term for social platforms one's audience is active on. This insight helps to guide you on the social platform to spend more time on building your influence.

Once again with a simple tool like *Buzzsumo.com* you will have this data. Simply put a keyword related to your niche and immediately it will show you the most shared content in that niche and the social media it is shared the most. For example, let's say you're blogging about passive income. You can see below that in the whole worldwide web the article with a passive income keyword with the highest engagement of 85.5K was written by theonion.com. The article was mostly shared on Facebook with Twitter and Reddit coming distant second and third respectively.

In the second position is an article from *yourfinancialtoolkit.com* with 17.6K engagement mostly from Pinterest. You can decipher from this insight that people who enjoy passive income topics are active on Facebook, Pinterest, and Twitter. If you're a passive income blogger, building your influence on these platforms with valuable content will bring you traffic.

This doesn't mean you can't experiment on other social platforms like Quora, Reddit, or LinkedIn. Far from it, you can experiment but prioritize platforms your target audience spends most of their time on.

DRIVING TRAFFIC TO YOUR BLOG | 73

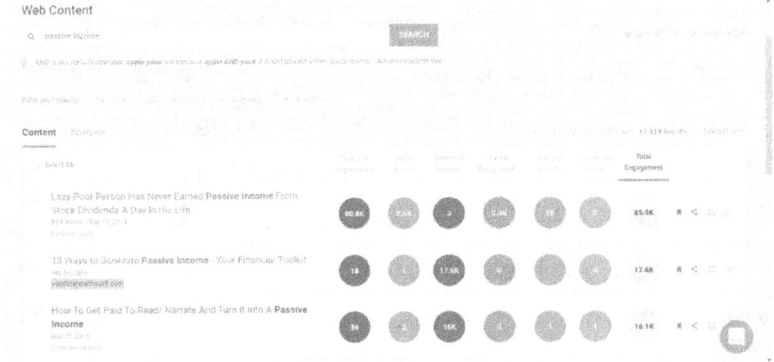

Courtesy: Buzzsumo.com

Free Traffic

Free traffic is traffic you acquire without monetary cost. It is also referred to as organic traffic. Since it is free monetary wise, it requires your time especially when it comes to generating traffic from search engines where you need to spend a good amount of time doing Search Engine Optimization on both your site and on each content that you publish. As for social media, you equally spend time building your followership and influence to drive traffic to your blog.

Search engines often generate the most traffic for bloggers so start as early as with your domain name - selecting a domain name that resembles your niche keyword, apply the SEO guidelines explained in Chapter 5, optimized each blog post as discussed in the last Chapter. Gradually you will start noticing tons of traffic from Google as it serves your optimized content to the relevant audience.

Whilst you are waiting on Google to index and start bringing you traffic which might take some time, a good place to start getting traffic from day one is social media platforms. Publish your content on your audience most visited platforms to start driving engagement and influence. If you consistently provide valuable content, people will notice and will share your content which will drive traffic to your blog. Creating relevant video content on *YouTube.com,* publishing some of your blogs on *Medium.com,* and answering questions on *Quora.com* are also known strategies that bring good quality traffic to your blog.

Paid Traffic

All the aforementioned social media platforms where you can get free traffic all have paid advertising features. Gone are the days when big companies with deep pockets are the only ones that can avoid marketing agencies with deep data analytics. With as little as $100 you can get started on Facebook using their Big Data to hyper-target potential readers and customers.

Their social media marketing dashboards might look daunting at the beginning but as you crush and learn to optimize your ads, they can be a gold mine honestly. Take for instance Facebook allows you to create targeted ads using various variables like *age, location, behavior, lookalike audience (clone of Facebook users who have similar characteristics like your website visitors), gender.* It is simply amazing.

Email List

If you have a mailing list, that will be a very good starting point in distributing and getting that much needed earlier eyeballs to your website. However for beginners, you can start curating your mailing lists using Facebook paid leads generation with lead magnets. Lead magnets are simply what you give someone to entice him or her to give you his or her email address. There are other free ways to build your mailing list like putting an opt-in form with a lead magnet in a visible area on your blog.

As a blogger, your email list is your greatest asset and you should start early to build it up. There are lots of good emailing marketing software in the market to get started with like Mailchimp, Convertkit, and Aweber.

Interview Industry Thought Leaders

This is another viable way to get lots of free traffic to your blog. Most times we think that captains of industries in our niche are unapproachable for interviews but you'd be amazed how many of them will be willing to talk to you if you just ask them.

Send out emails requesting an interview to thought leaders in your niche, and publish the interviews on your blog. Not only will the name recognition boost your credibility and increase traffic to your website, the interviewee will most probably share the content too, further expanding your blog reach.

Host Webinars

People love to learn, and combined with an effective social

promotion, webinars are an excellent way to impart your wisdom to your eagerly waiting audience and increase traffic to your website. Send out an email a week or so ahead of time, as well as a "last chance to register" reminder the day before the webinar. Make sure to record the presentation for later viewing, and promote your webinars widely through social media. There are several webinars platforms to choose from like *GoToWebcast, WebinarJam, GoToWebinar, Zoom, EverWebinar, GetResponse, Google Hangouts*, and a host of others.

Influencer Marketing

Influencer marketing is another great way to drive traffic to your new blog. Reach out to influencers on social media where your type of audience is most engaged be it Facebook, Instagram, or Twitter to leverage their popularity in sharing your content. Mind you this might not be free but it could potentially bring you huge traffic and put your blog out there.

Submit Your Content to Aggregator Sites

Aggregator sites like Reddit are a good place to submit your content. Reddit is a very popular website and records millions of visitors every day, you can piggy bank on this massive traffic by submitting your content in the relevant subreddit.

Don't spam Reddit and other similar sites. Members of communities like Reddit are extraordinarily savvy to spam disguised as legitimate links, but strive to add value in the ongoing discussion in the particular relevant subreddit you're targeting and watch the traffic pour in.

ACTION STEPS

Now you're aware that it doesn't end with crafting amazing content alone especially when you're starting. You need to get our content out there by implementing any or all the strategies discussed in this chapter.

BUILDING YOUR EMAIL LIST

Your greatest asset as a blogger is your email list. You might have a huge following on various social media - Facebook, Instagram, YouTube, and the rest but the fact remains that you don't own those audiences. Something as simple as a change of policy by the social media companies can adversely affect your business and income. There have been cases where social media companies have banned some individuals outright.

Building a huge followership on social media platforms is great but it's like having a huge party at someone's backyard. He can decide to kick you out anytime!

That's why it is extremely important to start building your email list from day one. Many bloggers take this for granted or postpone its implementation for too long.

Your email list is your number one asset, your go-to audience any day at any time. You have unfettered access to these people, with a click of a button you can instantly promote your blog posts to them without paying a cent!

Email marketing has continued to demonstrate outstanding ROI (Return on Investment). According to Campaign Monitor, Email marketing is the king in the marketing kingdom with a whopping 4400% ROI which translates to $44 for every $1 spent.

Disruptive Advertising statistics also showed that Shoppers spend 138% more when marketed to through email, as compared to those who do not receive email offers.

It is obvious that from the above statistics that email marketing trumps other forms of marketing and any blogger who is serious about blogging and marketing his content should prioritize email list building.

Let's delve deeper into the best strategies and management practices of building and maintaining an email list.

CREATING A LEAD MAGNET

Converting your website visitors into customers is not that easy. It's often a lengthy process, which requires constant persuasion and being on top of the mind of prospective customers (or leads). This process is what is referred to as Lead Nurturing, which starts with collecting leads.

The more the number of leads you collect from your blog, the higher is your chance of converting more customers.

So how do you increase the number of leads? One answer is by using lead magnets.

Lead magnets are critical to the success of lead generation strategy. We'll go into detail on the best practices of creating super effective highly converting lead magnets. But first, let's start with the definition of lead magnet.

What's a lead magnet? A lead magnet is something valuable that you provide to your visitors/readers in exchange for their contact details (usually, their email address) on a lead-gen form. A lead magnet can be anything: ebooks, whitepapers, research reports, eCommerce coupons, free access to an application, etc. If a lead magnet offers significant value, visitors fill in their contact information to receive that value.

Most certainly you have seen an email opt-in form on various websites that ask you to put your email address in exchange for a free offer that the website offers - it may be an ebook, a report, templates, or free email course. Whatever the offer is, most times if we find the freebie valuable enough we put our email to receive the freebie.

That is the principle of lead magnets.

Now that we are clear on what a lead magnet is, let's look at ways to build and optimize our lead magnet for maximum efficacy.

1. Keep Lead Magnets Targeted

A lead magnet has to be extremely targeted to be successful.

If you're offering a generic freebie on your form, you might end up collecting leads that are irrelevant to your business.

Consider this: If you are a men's beard grooming brand, releasing a guide on 'How to groom your beard' on Pinterest is not very likely to get you great leads because 80% of the audience on Pinterest are female.

Your lead magnet should target a specific group of your blog readers for better results. For example if your blog is about teaching people how to start blogging, you can create an ebook lead magnet on the first basic steps that one needs to take to start a blog and put it in strategic positions on your website.

2. Give a Glimpse of Your Content Beforehand

On your lead-gen form or click-through page, highlight points about how the lead magnet can provide tremendous value to readers. You can list out the broad headlines and a few actionable insights that your lead magnet covers to aid the reader in making that quick decision of giving you his or her email address to download it.

3. A/B Test Your Lead Magnets

A/B testing is essential in determining whether a lead magnet is working for you or not.

Even when a lead magnet is driving a significant number of leads to you, you cannot be sure if that is the best you can achieve.

A/B test In-Content lead magnet against a Sidebar lead magnet or a Pop-Up lead magnet.

Test to see if a glimpse (gist) of lead magnet on a form helps you increase conversions in comparison to a form with just an image of the lead magnet. Find out what is driving the conversions (the offering or the form design).

Test to find if a package of content works as a better lead magnet than a standalone content resource.

Apart from these ideas, you can also test the design, placement, and usability of your lead magnet forms.

4. Always Provide Top-Notch Content

Your lead magnet has to be greatly useful to your visitors. If your visitors don't find any value in the lead magnet, they won't develop a positive image of your brand. When your brand image suffers, so does your business. Even if a half-cooked lead magnet ends up delivering you a thousand leads, most leads might not convert at the end. Keep the following points in mind: Don't offer obsolete content resources. Deliver the exact resource which you promise on your lead-gen form. Offer content that is relevant to your typical website visitor. Make your content resources easily understandable.

5. Provide More Than Just eBooks

Sure, ebooks are a handy resource to give away. But what if your website visitors crave for something other than ebooks? What if other forms of resources related to your business and potential customers are better? It might be an email course that is relevant to your audience or swipe files.

Here is an extensive list of possible lead magnets segmented by audience type as provided by ConversionXL[17]:

Experts

- Ebooks and Whitepapers
- Mini-courses via email or Video series
- Audio recording, podcast
- Free course/webinar (free education in any format) Assessment or Test

E-commerce

- Free coupon
- Free shipping
- Gift with the first order

- Educational content on how to achieve/build stuff with what you sell
- Guide to saving money when shopping for X
- Membership (make prospects feel special, invite them into your VIP group that provides bonuses, advice etc)
- Educational material related to the need they will solve with your product.

Software

- Free trial
- Freemium account
- Demo

Service business

- Free coupons
- Educational content for DIY projects
- How to be a smart buyer of X
- Things you need to know before buying Y
- Free online tools (home decor planner, pet optimal nutrition calculator, car online custom tuning, etc.)

STRATEGIC POSITIONING OF YOUR EMAIL OPT-IN

After choosing your email service provider and creating your lead magnet, the next step is positioning your Email Opt-in at strategic positions on your website to achieve maximum conversion.

The place where the email opt-in is placed on your blog directly affects the number of subscribers that sign up to join your mailing list.

As soon as you finish your blog, place the email opt-in (which goes together with the lead magnet) at conspicuous places on your website like the top header of the homepage, at the end of every post (you get the idea) and sidebar of pages.

Hidden email opt-in forms barely get any subscriber, so once you have done the hard work and created the lead magnet, use Google Analytics to see your most visited pages and posts then place the lead magnet with the email opt-in form there. If you are just starting without any visitors data to rely on, then top header placement on your homepage and at the end of every blog post will suffice for now till you start getting data insights from Google Analytics.

Designing your email opt-in form to beautifully pop out is also part of strategic positioning. Use warm colors that contrast your brand theme color to design your email opt-in forms so it can be eye-catching and attention-grabbing. Adobe Color Wheel is a good tool for selecting complementary and contrasting colors.

Another good method of placing email opt-in is using exit pop up email opt-in forms. They are those email opt-ins you may have seen pop up on various websites as you're about to leave the website. It is like a last-minute final try to get your visitor to opt-in on your mailing list. It is known to have a high conversion rate and I highly recommend it.

EMAIL LIST MANAGEMENT

Email list management is the practice of segmenting and tagging your email contacts according to their behaviors, interests, and engagements with your site.

Your segmentation and tagging might look something like this;

- Blog subscribers
- Customers
- Trial users
- Lead magnet downloaders
- Purchased an offer

This allows for easy identification of different subscriber groups for laser-focused email marketing. Imagine having two different lead magnets A and B on your website, you will like to automatically tag new email contacts as they download a specific lead magnet. For example people that downloaded lead magnet A will be tagged something like Readers that downloaded lead magnet A and people that downloaded lead magnet B will be tagged Readers that downloaded lead magnet B.

These special tags will help you to easily manage your email list and nurture them towards your offer according to their interests which they have earlier indicated to you through their choice of lead magnets.

Keeping your email lists organized can save you a lot of time that you can spend on what is more important like the creation of your email nurturing sequence which is sent automatically as soon as one subscribes. There are various email marketing software in the market that are good but I use and recommend Convertkit because it is built for creators and bloggers.

ACTION STEPS

Your email list is your greatest asset as a blogger, set it up from day one and use it to develop warm relationships with your readers.

SECTION 3 - MONETIZATION

BLOG MONETIZATION METHODS

In this chapter, we are going to discuss various methods for monetizing a blog. Traffic is very important in blog monetization but it's not the only factor. For any blog to have a good prospect of making money in the fiercely competitive blog industry, that blog must obey the Five Cardinal Rules of Blogging.

5 CARDINAL RULES OF BLOGGING.

Before I proceed with the various ways you can monetize your blog, whether you just started the blog or you've had it for some time now, I want to firstly cover the five cardinal rules of blogging. If you pay attention to these laws, you'll succeed over time. Ignore them, and you'll find it nearly impossible to drive any respectable amount of traffic and ultimately monetize your blog.

1. Focus

Blogs need focus. You need to have a specific industry, niche or topic that you write about repeatedly. Don't be all over the map. You'll find that veering off on tangents will make you lose your core audience. People want to visit a blog and keep revisiting it because it fulfills their needs. That happens by staying focused and on topic. Once you have researched and picked your niche, stick to it!

2. Quality

People think that blogging is about pushing out an enormous amount of content. But it doesn't work if it's thin content. You need to go for quality instead of quantity. Your content needs to be quality content. It needs to be thorough, well-written, and designed. If a study is referenced, it needs to be cited and linked to. Don't skimp on quality if you're serious about monetizing your blog.

3. Value

Your blog needs to deliver value. People don't care about your motive for starting the blog, they care and pay for value. What can you teach other people about? What are you an expert at? Take the time to deliver value. Creating thorough tutorials and informative posts that interweave things like videos and other media to truly help people understand or figure something out. Value is a precursor to income in any industry, but especially in blogging.

4. Engagement

How engaging is your content? Does your blog incite people to spend a lot of time reading articles, watching videos, or messaging on a forum, for example? The more people engage with your content, the more likely they'll be to purchase something from you. Without engagement, there's very little chance of monetization. This is where you unleash your creativity to get readers to stay longer on your site. Designing a captivating blog post that mixes the right colors and images is one of the ways to foster engagement.

5. Authority

People naturally prefer to be taught by an expert. So how much authority do you have? How well-known are you in your field? The more authority you have, the more likely you can monetize your blog quickly. For example, if you have a large social media following and you decide to launch a blog, you can drive traffic quickly. If you're an expert at something else or a best-selling author, for example, you already have authority, all you need to do is leverage it.

BLOG MONETIZATION.

While there are various methods to monetize your blog, these eight methods are the core monetization techniques of any blog. But before we delve into that, It is important to know that your blog is just there to attract potential customers with great content you are churning out. It's when readers land on your site that your behind the scene Sales Machine starts to work on autopilot to implement any of the below monetization methods as the case may be.

1. Affiliate marketing

One of the most popular methods for monetizing a blog is to leverage affiliate marketing. It is marketing and selling a third party product for a commission. This is especially useful when you're just starting and you don't have your products or services to sell. To utilize this method, all you have to do is to develop content that is in sync or explains whatever the affiliate offers that you plan to promote.

For example, if you're running a food blog, you can easily register with Amazon Associates (Amazon's affiliate program) to sell cooking utensils and related products. Since the content is already attracting people that are interested in food, selling these types of products helps you to create a near-automated stream of passive income.

Other affiliate networks a beginner blogger can join to start making money immediately are ClickBank, ShareASale, CJ Affiliate, etc.

2. Advertisements

While most people might think that adding some pay-per-click

(PPC) ads will be a great way to make lots of money with their blogs, unless you have massive amounts of traffic -- as in 10,000+ visitors per day or more -- the income will be marginal at best.

With the average revenue for a thousand banner ad views, industry-wide, at $2.80 (and dropping all the time). And considering that you're likely to go through an ad network of some kind who will take around 30% of the revenue, that means you're getting about 70% of it. Which means for 1,000 views on your site, you make around $1.96. It doesn't take a math wizard to see the tragedy of that one. Plus, so much of it depends on the market, so many bloggers earn far less than even that. The real income here doesn't start until you cross about 100,000 visitors per day.

However, you could easily negotiate terms directly with advertisers by utilizing display ads as opposed to PPC ads. As long as the ads are within your specific niche or industry, you can likely negotiate an amount that would be much more competitive than income from standard PPC ads.

3. Email marketing

As discussed in the last chapter, one of the most powerful methods for making money from your blog is directly through email marketing. But to be successful, you need to build your list. As many might make you believe that your email marketing profitability is directly related to the size of your list, this is untrue. Your email list profitability isn't dependent on the size of your list but on how you nurture and nudge your subscribers to your offer.

By building a strong bond and a connection with your readers, you can effectively generate a sizable amount of money through the course of marketing both your products and services along with affiliate offers directly through email. You can expect to generate approximately $1 per subscriber per month.

Email marketing can be automated with various Email SaaS (Software as a Service) like Mailchimp, Convertkit, Aweber, and others.

4. Sell ebooks

Ebooks offer a relatively quick pathway for making money from your blog. Develop an ebook that's aligned with the content of your blog. Non-fiction ebooks are relatively simple to create, and if you're teaching a skill that many people struggle with, the ebook will likely produce a healthy profit.

You can easily promote your ebook directly through your blog by creating attractive content that will draw people in, then enticing them with your ebook. You could also build a sales funnel, which is an online marketing term for an automated multi-step sales machine, and sell your ebook on autopilot.

5. Sell courses

Selling digital online courses is another way you can profit from blogging. Create intuitive and helpful courses that add a tremendous amount of value and the rest will be smooth sailing. By putting your heart and your soul into these courses, you can simply allow them to sell on autopilot for you, another great avenue for passive income.

Courses work great when it comes to technical skills like web development, digital marketing, graphic design, and so on. But they also work in formats like finances, stocks, currency investing, and accounting. The key is finding what you're great at and doing market research to validate that there is a need for your course before building the course. Then make something far better than the other courses out there in the marketplace.

6. Sell digital products

Creating digital products is a great way to profit from your blog. You can effectively sell any type of digital information product on your blog as long as it's in harmony with your content. You can build a webinar to market your product and deliver them through a member's area or other downloadable means.

Digital products can be a combination of videos, downloadable guides, resources, PDFs, software components, SaaS, and others. Do your best to create something that helps fill a need. Don't second guess yourself, as you'd be surprised at just how much money you can make by selling digital products on your blog.

7. Sell coaching services

While it does seem like coaching services are infiltrating every aspect of the market these days, selling coaching services through your blog can be a lucrative prospect. Whether you set yourself up as a life coach, a career coach, or a business development coach, you can earn a significant income through just a handful of clients.

Decide on your course modules, and do your best to ensure that you address any objections upfront. Customers tend to abandon the purchase process when it's too complicated.

8. Secure sponsorships

Sponsorships are a great way to make money from your blog but it is not for beginners, you need the traffic if you're going to sell it for a significant amount of money. You can create sponsored posts as long as you label them as sponsored. The FTC cracks down on marketing products and services, including articles that are sponsored when in fact they're passed off as organic.

You have to be careful with sponsorships. Be sure that you're upfront with your readership. Google also cares acutely about sponsored links and will penalize you if you're selling links along with penalizing the site that you're linking to. Simply put, it's not worth it, so be as transparent as possible if you want to use this method.

ACTION STEPS

Whatever method you choose, just ensure that it aligns with the content of your blog. As a beginner I recommend starting with affiliate marketing, then proceed to create your small entry priced (not more than $29) digital products like templates, swipe files, etc. The response of your audience will then inform your graduation to develop a course which you can host on Thinkific.com[18] or Teachable and sell on autopilot.

11

HOW TO MAKE SELLING NATURAL AND NOT ANNOYING TO YOUR AUDIENCE

Most bloggers fall into this trap of becoming a sleazy salesperson abusing their email contacts with a constant bombardment of sales pitch. To make things worse, they don't even nurture the potential customers that subscribe to their list before sending them endless sales pitches. This type of action no doubt leads to incessant email list unsubscription.

For someone to land on your blog and subscribe to your email list doesn't mean that he or she is ready yet to buy from you. The person is still a cold prospect. He still needs to be primed and warmed up to your brand and what you have to offer.

This is where email marketing does its magic. From the time that the subscriber enters your list, you can set an email sequence that welcomes him and introduces you, and for days keeps nurturing your prospect by providing a ton of value to the prospect.

This automatic email sequence amongst other things achieves one vital thing that is so important in marketing - Top of mind

Top of mind is simply using various marketing techniques (email marketing works best for bloggers) to stay on the prospect's mind always for your type of service in order to be considered first when the prospect is ready to make a purchase.

Now let's look at the ways you can increase sales on your blog without being sleazy or pushy.

1. Make that first connection impressive and memorable

As the cliche goes you don't have a second chance to make another first impression. So seize the moment and make your first impression with your potential customer memorable.

Selling is all about relationships. When you take the time to connect with someone before you share your offers, it shows a genuineness that customers are often drawn to. Nothing feels worse than when it seems as if someone only cares about your money, so make sure you don't make your potential clients feel like that. The most important part of the sales process is the rapport building -- don't skip over it.

Use your email marketing software to send all new subscribers a welcome email immediately they join your mailing list. Then follow it up with an email sequence that will usher in the nurturing process- giving the prospect free tips and guidelines to solve his immediate problem or achieve the transformation that he envisions. It is only after this warm rapport that you can be able to pitch him your offer.

2. Don't sell product or service, sell transformation

The simple truth is that customers buy transformations and not products or services. A customer is interested in how your product or service will help him transform from his miserable Point A (pain point location) to happy Point B (pain-free location).

Hence make your marketing message clear by highlighting the potential customer's pain point and how your product or service solves it.

It is always better to craft a blog post with the sole aim of promoting an offer. A well-written content serves as the lead magnet, in this case, to attract leads to the offer. So when you're writing the content ask yourself: Why should my ideal client care? The answer to that question will likely give you some guidance on how you can market to your clients.

It's easy to get into the habit of talking about what you're selling rather than why you're selling it. Make sure you're not falling into this trap. Some helpful ways to ensure you're focusing on the "why" include talking about the transformation that clients can expect in your marketing content and sharing client results and testimonials.

3. Keep the focus on them not you

At the end of the day, customers want to know how your product or service can affect them. That's more important to them than hearing about how it has affected you. For instance, a customer will care much more about how a face wash will clear their acne rather than how it cleared yours. Remember this simple point when you're engaging in conversations with potential clients, and be sure to keep the focus on them.

4. Don't follow up too often

You want to get in touch with a prospect as soon as possible, which means sending them a welcome email and putting them on a nurturing email sequence. However within your email nurturing or follow up sequence, give some days say two days interval before the email software sends the next email in your pre-programmed emails. It's always important to ask the customer about his progress since your last email, this makes the customer genuinely believe that you care and increases his trust for you.

5. Use data insights to refine your engagement

Leverage the data insights reported by your email marketing

software to understand your leads very well to craft what the next engagement will be.

All email marketing software provides information about contacts that opened your email or clicked on a link embedded in the mail. Use this information to tag and segment your subscribers to serve them better and increase your sales conversion rate.

Example: You can create a mini quiz to better segment your email list. A simple quiz like below will help you see the subset of your list that are interested in traffic generation and building backlinks.

Quiz Sample

What is your blogging greatest challenge now?

1. *Traffic generation*
2. *Building backlinks*

As the subscribers answer the quiz, your email software should be able to automatically tag and segment them at the backend making it easier for you to keep engaging your subscribers with the most relevant content.

ACTION STEPS

Use your email marketing software to do the heavy

lifting here. Simply craft a beautiful content that highlights the problem the potential customer is facing and the solution your offer is bringing. Then create an email series that will take over the nurturing of subscribers once they enlist on your mailing list and gradually nudge them to make a purchase.

CONCLUSION

Your blog is like an iceberg, the small visible portion that is afloat is your site, then the larger portion that is submerged is your background sales machine - your lead magnets, email marketing system, and your core offers.

Right from the start, your blog should be treated as a business system, not just a website to post content that attracts social share or comments from readers. Instead, it should be the central magnetic hub where you publish highly valuable content that is aligned with your major offer to attract leads/potential customers.

Use your email marketing software to move captured leads through your sales funnel to convert them to paying customers.

Remember the gas that fuels your blog is traffic, always refer to Chapter 5 for actionable steps on how to increase your traffic.

Finally remember to fetch your patience robe from your washing line and wear it, lol because blogging will test your patience level to the limit as you start. But don't despair, continue to implement all you have read and over time you will start seeing some traffic which will snowball to a big audience if you keep your consistency and always post targeted valuable content.

Never neglect the power of dreams to keep you going. Always make out some time once in a few weeks to daydream about why you want to start a blog. Is it because you want to have freedom of time while earning full-time income which your 9 to 5 job can't afford? Or you want a passive income source that will be able to pay for your lifestyle and enable you to quit your job. Maybe you want to use it to build your influence as an authority in your industry.

Whatever the reason might be, always take some time to daydream for a few minutes how sweet the realization of this dream will be. Imagine yourself and your family taking that vacation on a lovely island and your blog is busy minting money on autopilot without your effort! It is always a refreshing exercise I normally embark on and it keeps me focused.

With all that being said, it is now time to take that action step of buying a web host, setting up your blog and start creating those awesome contents.

Before you go, remember to download your bonuses at https://tovalezeani.com/make-money-blogging-on-wordpress-bonus-pack/[19].

THANK YOU FOR READING

I hope you enjoyed reading this book. With many things begging for our time these days, I really appreciate you taking your time to read this book and will love to hear from you. Could you please leave me a review on Amazon letting me know what you thought of the book? Thank you so much! If you want to get in touch, come find me here at my own corner of the internet: https://www.tovalezeani.com[20].

Toval

ABOUT THE AUTHOR

Toval is a blogger, entrepreneur, and Microsoft Certified Information Technology Professional. He loves publishing informative contents and tips on how beginners can start and scale their blogs profitably on his renowned blog - Tovalezeani.com

When he is not blogging, he is passionate about exploring the world with his Sony Camera.

REFERENCES

COPYRIGHT PAGE

1. https://tovalezeani.com/booklinks

INTRODUCTION PAGE

2. https://tovalezeani.com/make-money-blogging-on-wordpress-bonus-pack/

CHAPTER 1

3. https:/adwords.google.com/home/tools/keyword-planner/
4. https://ahrefs.com/
5. https://www.semrush.com/sem/?ref=2534382083&refer_source=&utm_source=berush&utm_medium=promo&utm_campaign=link_7-day_pro_trial

CHAPTER 2

6. https://www.bluehost.com/track/valezeani/
7. https://www.bluehost.com/track/valezeani/

CHAPTER 3

8. https://wordpress.org/download/
9. https://filezilla-project.org/
10. https://www.bluehost.com/track/valezeani/

CHAPTER 5

11. https://www.semrush.com/lp/all-in-one-marketing-toolkit/en/?ref=2534382083&refer_source=&utm_source=berush&utm_medium=promo&utm_campaign=link_landing_page:_all-in-one_marketing_toolkit

12. https://search.google.com/search-console/welcomehttps://search.google.com/search-console/welcome

13. https://www.semrush.com/lp/all-in-one-marketing-toolkit/en/?ref=2534382083&refer_source=&utm_source=berush&utm_medium=promo&utm_campaign=link_landing_page:_all-in-one_marketing_toolkit

CHAPTER 6

14. https://contentmarketinginstitute.com/2019/10/success-differentiators-b2b-research/

CHAPTER 7

15. https://coschedule.com/headline-analyzer
16. https://www.aminstitute.com/headline/

CHAPTER 9

17. https://cxl.com/blog/lead-magnets-email-list-building-on-steroids/

CHAPTER 10

18. http://try.thinkific.com/tovalezeani5130

CONCLUSION

19. https://tovalezeani.com/make-money-blogging-on-wordpress-bonus-pack/
20. https://www.tovalezeani.com

www.ingramcontent.com/pod-product-compliance
Lightning Source LLC
Chambersburg PA
CBHW071418210526
45465CB00001B/447